THE BOOK OF CAB O[VERS]

by Ted Campbell and his trucking buddies from all over the world

For many years in North America most state and provincial laws limited overall truck length to 42 feet on major highways. Setting the cab over the engine shaved length off the tractor, which were added to the trailer, keeping the dimensions legal and carrying more cargo. Cabovers caught on in the between the 1950's and 1970's as America's Interstate Highway System expanded and truck lengths increased. It took several years for some states and provinces to ease their laws regarding over-all vehicle length.

Canada was slower to adopt the RTAAC rules.

Consolidated Freightways management were both motivated and innovative, in 1953 they built the WF64, a sleeper cab with the bunk over top of the cab. The following year they produced a four-wheel-drive, the WF6344T, an ad is shown on page 62.

Competition caught on fast, Mack, Kenworth, Peterbilt, International, Ford, General Motors, Dodge, Hayes, Marmon, produced cab over's and improved on them.

There is a nostalgia among us "old school" truckers, we look back fondly on the trucks and time of an era we know will never return.

KEN DUBUC – St. Paul Alberta

This is a great, start-to-finish story about a 1979 Peterbilt 400 Cummins 15 speed over transmission Eaton 3:90 200" wheel base brown interior some cool history is that this was ordered as a show truck for the Peterbilt dealer the colours were beige and different shades of green I was told of this at the Calgary Peterbilt store from a parts guy. It was a show truck and now it's a show truck again. I can put the names to all that owned this truck at one point I sold it to Greg Elko then my friend Art Kleckner bought it and ran to the east coast. He sold it to a bull hauler Brian Sandy then I believe it was at the Calgary public auction Mike Yorikow from Vegreville then to Grande Prairie, Innisfree to a Dwayne Fowler then to present home in Saint Paul as a show truck.

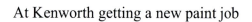

At Kenworth getting a new paint job

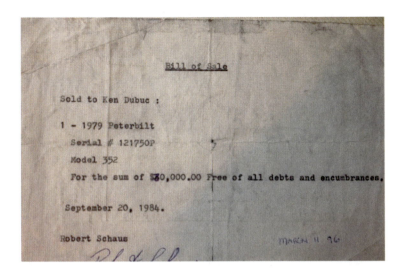

KEN DUBUC'S BILL OF SALE. Back in the day people trusted people.

The Pete as a "collector item"
near it's present home Saint Paul Alberta

TED CAMPBELL Langley BC

3406 @ 425 13 speed, 46,000 diffs,

Somewhere back in time it was leased on with Day & Ross I found a safety pamphlet inside. This 1987 IHC was piggy-backed to Western Star Trucks Langley in June of 1990 with twenty other trucks when a Winnipeg dealership folded. I took a good look at them, the IHC was the best of the lot but when I opened the door I gagged. Someone had peed the mattress, summer heat made the smell atrocious. Next time Larry Farney, the considerably over-weight Associates Finance Manager came to our office he and I did a walk-around. I opened the COE door. "Climb up there, get a whiff of that. Someone peed the mattress, if you give us a P.O to clean it and a new mattress we can get around $35,000.00 for it." He shook his head."I ain't climbing no ladder and I ain't putting a dime in none of them." It sat for months. Not only did we not get an offer, prospective buyers never even started the engine. Late in August I walked into a restaurant, Larry was in front of me."When are you going to buy that COE from me?" I do not normally carry a cheque book but I happened to have one that day. I used his back as a desk, wrote a cheque for $12,000.00 to Associates, handed it to him. He read it. "What about the sales tax?" I replied. "Make up the Bill of Sale, I'll give you the extra." "It'll be ready this afternoon." I rolled the windows down, put on rubber gloves, threw the mattress in the garbage container, used Bleach and Pine Sol, put in the best mattress money could buy. Cat had a package deal on 3406 bearings and a water pump. I put on eight fresh recaps and two new steers. Hired Rob Towpich to drive it, leased it on with Gary Cassidy's Michawn Carriers out of Aldergrove BC on the California produce run. When I left Gary it was the first truck when I started Pure Water Transport.

My Grandson Jason, age 9, "start 'em young they'll turn out right" He did

THE DOMAN FLEET Duncan and Richmond BC

MH Mack, E-9 @ 450, Mack 12 speed, Mack 38,000. Roy was heading west up the Princeton hill in BC, with a full load of lumber crossed the Whipsaw Creek bridge, put his toe into it to get a run at the Mine hill, laid it on its left side. I was in my office at Mainland Mack when I got the call. "I laid it over on the XXXXX hill, I'm in the hospital with broken ribs.
Can you come for me?"
I realized I wasn't sure if he said Princeton or Creston.
Scattered lumber on the Princeton Mine Hill was a giveaway.

MORE DOMAN COE'S

The numbers told a story 310 was the 10th truck bought in 1983

When Herb Doman bought a truck his shop crew put a "Doman Log-end" decal on each door. It never came off, once a Doman truck always a Doman truck.
The very first Doman truck was a 1952 Dodge. The air system,
must have been added later by the shop crew for use as a yard truck

CASEY ALLEN Millville Texas

1986 Kenworth K100
It's power train is 400 hp big cam4 NTC Cummins. 13 speed. 3:55 rears. 196"wb. 630,000 actual miles. For the last 10 years it's been pulling bullracks and grain hoppers. I'm still trying to run down work history from before. I bought it to restore but it's already nice, it's basically only gonna get fresh paint, stacks and hopefully dual breathers. About myself, I've been trucking for just under 20 years. I try to restore one truck a year after I've driven it for a while to get the mechanical back in shape. I love old vintage trucks. Before being a trucker I was a body man and painter so restoring these are my passion.

FRED POLINDER and JUSTIN MORGAN
Lynden and Custer Wa.

Justin Morgan Custer Wa.

Fred Polinder and Justin Morgan at the Paccar Technical Centre, Mt. Vernon Wa.
Fred was a long time driver for Lynden Transport, on the Alaska run then on milk tankers.
He has a large collection of oldie but goodies in a specially built pole-barn at Lynden Wa.

cool old combo 55 Kenworth 62 Wilson

DARREL SOFRANIUK a.k.a. King of the Highway
Winnipeg Manitoba

IF IT'S A DARREL SOFRANIUK TRUCK IT'S A CABOVER

DEAN MHYRE – Dauphin Manitoba

I bought this 1979 352 from Howie Hildebrand in 2009, he saved it from the pasture.
It came new with an 8V92, 15 over and 4.11 gears. I switched it to a 3406B cat
and 18 speed. I got my class one in 2002, purchased my first truck that year also
a 1990 Peterbilt 379. I've owned quite a few trucks ranging in age from 1979 - 2007
generally buying. fixing up, running a bit then selling and starting on the next one.
This is the only one I've had that I won't sell.
It hauls livestock steady, about 3000-3500 miles a week during cattle season

RAY SIDELLA – New Ringgold, Pa.
MACK CABOVERS

MH Mack I bought about 4 years ago out of Illinois.
I think it was originally a dealer stock item, sold to a farmer.
When I bought it it was original and white with blue stripes.
I sold it to a man who painted it Orange to match his fleet.
He sold it to a man that bought my Superliner who threw it in with the trade.
So I go it back. 1987 MH613 E6 350 9 spd 4.42 on neway air.
This is my 3rd MH. Had two V8 trucks back in The 90's.

My first MH e9 400 9 spd. 3leaf. 188wb.
Turned it up. Stretched to 240 with Neway

PAUL DOWNING - 1977 White Freightliner

Hi Ted Campbell yes that would be great!! It was a 1977 White Freightliner Greensboro paint scheme it had a small Cummins power I believe 280 hp My dad ran all over Canada and the states with it.
My dad's name was Les Downing. Thanks Ted!! Paul Downing

STEVE BARCLAY – Brechin Ontario

Erb had the coolest trucks back in the day
this Freightliner was at the Markham truck show in 1988

DAVE ALDRICH = NEW ZEALAND

MALCOM J0NES
Here's a story that starts with a Cab Over
It is so good more should be told.
Malcom Jones owns this Peterbilt Cab Over
pulling a custom-built trailer.

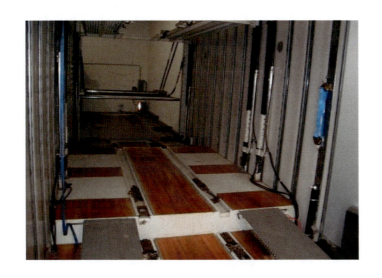

TODD CAMPBELL of KNOX CARRIERS

ICY RED - One of the best-known Cab Overs on Face Book

Todd Campbell has this Kenworth sitting outside the ToyBox
Hope she's patient.
All my trucks are she's. It's the way that it is.
This one is a '94 with a DDEC4 series 60 Detroit
and a decent wheelbase. Gotta make a few changes and repairs

KEVIN YOUNG

CAM HILTZ - 1968 GM CRACKERBOX

1st Runner-up
"Furniture A-Go-Go"

tractor of the month
Runners-Up

ROADMASTER Pres Higgins of Covina, California leases this metallic blue and white 1968 Jimmy to KKW Trucking.
Hauling new furniture within California is made a lot easier, thanks to a 318 Detroit Diesel and RTO 915 trans. The rear end is an Eaton 4:33 model.
Other items for this good looking cabover include a Mercury sleeper, Mark IV air conditioner, an air ride seat, an all-black upholstered interior, and power steering.
Tires for this rig are Firestone 10:00 x 20's. Chrome can best be seen in the mirrors, stacks, spotlights, grab handles, hub caps on the drive axles, and air horns. All wheels on the tractor are polished aluminum — wheels on the 1969 Fruehauf are chrome!
KKW Trucking has approximately 25 pieces of equipment, eight of which are leased. Twenty-four year old Dennis Firestone is the owner of this company, who's "bag" is hauling new furniture from manufacturer to retail outlets. The run is between Los Angeles and San Francisco.
The Los Angeles factory branch of GMC was the dealer that sold this rig to Mr. Higgins.

Photo by: OVERDRIVE

DENNIS DEXTER REED – Elsberry, Missouri

I'm a 3 truck agricultural hauler based out of Elsberry Mo. hauling wood products and grain for local farmers I'm my only driver, I do most of my own repairs and maintenance. The two older trucks were my Grandpa's and Dad's when we had Reed livestock out of Dexter Mo. Grandpa bought and sold hogs for Reelfoot pork out of Memphis, Dad started out hauling from Dexter to Memphis on a regular basis.
Both my 9670's are 1987 models with 400 big cam Cummins and 13 spd.

STEVE COLLINS – Vancouver BC

Green is a 1980, Black is a 1981 362 CAT 3408 DITA 15 over and 4:11's

Steve Collins 1980 362 with 3408 Cat

NORM BOULIANNE - Kapuskasing Ontario

It varies when it was green from the dryer kiln 63,500 we were legal but it was always over. The worst load was Montreal half load in Quebec and I had the centre core of the balsam tree that was heavy, 44 thousand feet rough lumber, when 39 thousands feet was legal.

You can't do that no more.

JOHN GOLDIE – 1980 Kenworth K-100

3408 15 Over on Dash 3.90 on 11R24.5 on Kenworth 8 bag suspension
Four 120 gallon tanks – 2 for fuel, 1 for hydraulics,
1 for wash water for truck shows
Back window VIT Interior

This was originally John's Fathers Tractor

LESLIE MADIGAN – Lancaster Ontario

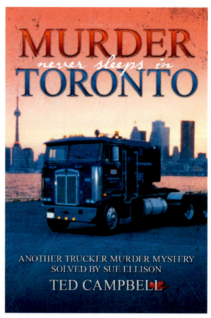

K-100 on Toronto Waterfront. 1988 Kenworth K100e 112" cab, 335 Cummins, 15 over on 11R24/.5. Former Earl Paddock tractor. – note the CN Tower in the background. I liked this tractor and picture so much I used it on the front cover of a Sue Ellison Mystery

This Argosy is Leslie's personal truck.

TIM LANGENBERG – Fonthill, Ontario
HEAVY HAULER

MADISON TULLY – Warren Manitoba
1986 FREIGHTLINER

Cat 3406B 13 Speed Dana-Spicer @ 3.90 Peterbilt lowleaf 206 wheelbase

1979 with A model Cat, 270" WB VIT Interior

GAGE SAILOR - WELLS MINNESOTA

Old girl waiting for better weather so so she can come outside and play

LEE HOWARD   Hampton Ontario

1998 KENWORTH 100E 600 hp Detroit, 18 speed

C J HALL - Oakville Ontario

C J Hall Freightliner Stretched with extra axle

MARVIN GERBRAND - Crystal City Manitoba

1981 Freightliner, 400B Cat, 15 Over, 3.70 ratio
Contracted to Glenn Sharpe
Based in Crystal City Manitoba
Ran on the California to Manitoba Produce run

DAVID EARL GAINEY

1975 Mack F-Model with 5 speed badly needing a bit of TLC

ERIC DAVIS - SKIDMORE Mo.

1996 Kenworth K-100 N-14 18 Speed   Factory back window

Ted Campbell collection new 1987 Mack MH 550 / 12 speed, Mack 38's on Neway at Ev's Truckport, Langley BC

BOB ABBOTT Roseto Pa.

Mack MH Owned by Bob Abbott, Roseto Pa. 1993 Mack MH 600
350 4 valve Mack motor. 9 speed road ranger. Reyco suspension
212000 miles

Ordered by Charles Karper Trucking, Chambersburg Pa. Driven by 1 driver til about 2012. Purchased by a private owner and stored. In 2015 a guy in Boston Mass. purchased it, ran for 2 years pulling a van to Florida, Oregon, Maine and New England. I bought it in March, 2018 to pull my 5th wheel and show use.

RON DENAULT Chemainus BC

Transportation . Ran the 401 corridor pulling B trains Ontario Quebec Michigan Ohio New York Second Owner RG Denault Transport.

MICHAEL ALAMORIAN COLLECTION – Union New Jersey

1981 GMC Astro 95 6V92TTA Detroit Diesel 335 HP.
9 speed Road Ranger Transmission . Based out of Newark,
NJ this truck hauled mostly empty cans and glass bottles
North to Merrimack NH, south to Jacksonville, Fl
west to Columbus , Ohio and all points in between

JIM ROSS – Milton West Virginia
1984 PETERBILT

1984 Cabover Pete 400 cat 13 speed. It was my first truck as an owner operator.
The last time I saw it was at a truck dealer in Ky around 2000.

BARRY SCOTT KEITH

'77 Peterbilt 350 Cummins 13 speed

MORGAN WAGONER - Butterfield Missouri

Ted Campbell here's my 1986 9670 international Cabover with a 350 big cam Cummins, Eaton 13 speed transmission with 4:11 Rockwell rears. My dad got the truck when he owned JR's truck repair in Tulsa, Oklahoma where he swapped the engine and wasn't paid for his work. He later stretched the frame in the late 90s I don't know who the original owner was. At one time the truck was least to Walt Disney entertainment. Now she pulls a walking floor or sometimes a flatbed under my own authority. Please keep me updated on the book. Thank you

GREGG HOFFMAN - Bangor Pennsylvania

My first MH was an E9-450, excellent truck. T2090, wish I had a 12-speed.

Happy with my current ride, E6 350-4v. 10-speed Road Ranger, still wishing I had a 12-speed.

STEHPEN AINEY – Whitby Ontario

These are the Mack MHs we restored, worked and sold to happy homes. The first one started as a blue 1989 MH from Western Canada E9500 Whispering Giant (sooo quiet) TRTXL1070B 12 speed Mack trans Mack 12f 40r on Camel back 417gears 24.5 steel wheels went like heck and passed everything but a fuel station. We purchased the truck as it had been sitting in Cambridge Macks backyard forever. The owner had passed away, we purchased it from his wife out west. It was put to work for a company I was working with. Sold it to buy my first house. (Should have found a big enough cardboard box instead) Next MH was a 1985 ex Panavision movie truck they retired, E6350 4V, 15 speed Fuller Mack 12 front and 40diffs on Neway 4.17 ratio 24.5 alum wheels. 220" wheelbase as it had a dromebox gen set on it. It went to a collector in FL. Look forward to another MH to restore.

DOUG ANDERSON Rainy River Ontario

Here's the 1980 K100C I used to own Ted.
I bought it in Or. 290,000 original miles.
It had a 350 Big Cam2 Cummins, rto9513 trans, SQHD 38000 Rears
Gentle is the word, when you let the clutch out.
I've since sold it to goods hands in Edmonton Ab.

THE SIGN ON THE FRONT BUMPER MEANS WHAT IT SAYS

1995 Peterbilt 362
N-14 18 Speed
Super 40's
Someone knew what
they were doing

1978 Peterbilt 352 being restored

1995 Peterbilt 362

From BILL AITCHISON on behalf of
GORDON ROBINSON – AN OLD-SCHOOL TRUCKER

Gordon Robinson – A Good Ole Boy

Gordy is the definition of a classic trucker. With a Class 1 drivers license since he was 18 years old, Gordy has been driving truck all over North America his entire adult life.

"I've trucked for more than 50 years and had a lot of fun," he says. "I've been in every state – as far North as Prudoe Bay, from Newfoundland to Victoria and all the way to the Mexican border."

> "I've had a good life. As long as I can get around, I'll keep working."

When Gordy retired (and he uses that word very loosely) and went on pension, he didn't want to have his pension reduced by working...too much. So he parked his truck for the winter and went back out to the job he knows best every spring. It was around that time that Barry called him and asked him what he was doing.

"He asked if I was interested in coming to move snow during the winter. I said yes and when spring came, I went back on the road."

When the "idiots" on the road, and the rules and regulations that grew over the course of his career, became more then he wanted to deal with, Gordy decided it was time to sell his truck. But he continued working at Beaver Trucks year round.

"I like working," he says with his well known mischievous smile. "And this is easy work for me."

And clearly, he likes being around trucks and the trucking world he spent his life in. For the last five years, he has moved trucks around for the salesmen, tested trucks for Howard and pushed snow in the winter.

Gordy doesn't take holidays and even at home, Gordy is always doing something. Married 52 years this fall to Eleanor, they have two children, Doreen and Wayne and four grandchildren between the ages of 15 and 22 who he enjoys visiting with.

The small acreage he and his wife own in St Francis Xavier gives him the opportunity to work around the property cutting grass. He also enjoys tuning up his lawnmower and the lawnmowers of some of the guys from the office, and puttering around his shop.

Despite two hip replacements, at the age of 73, Gordy still moves like a young man, walking with a skip in his step, testament to his enjoyment of life in general and his time at work.

"I've had a good life. As long as I can get around, I'll keep working."

Hey Ted, this is Gordon Robinson and a few of his trucks. He lives in Winnipeg Mb. Now retired. He did all his own wrenching and taught many of us younger guys how to be good truckers.

BILL AITCHISON'S FATHER'S 1970 FREIGHTLINER
Built in Vancouver BC.

BOB ROAD-BOSS PETTIT Hartselle Alabama

DENNIS JOHNSON – Clark South Dakota

GLENN BRENDEL

YOU WANT CABOVERS – I'LL SHOW YOU CABOVERS

EVEL KNIEVEL JUMPING A WHOLE BUNCH OF CABOVERS

EXPRESSWAYS VANCOUVER SOLD TO Canadian Pacific in 1958
BULLNOSE KENWORTH AND HALFSHACK KENWORTH
BOTH HAD 220 CUMMINS 5 & 3

HIGHWAY HANK – Welland Ontario
2003 KW K100E

Factory N14 @ 470 hp 10 spd transmission 232" wheelbase
Was ordered, and ran in the U.S. as a boat hauler.
Eventually made its way to Canada, where the new owner made it a mini bus hauler
(little yellow buses from Thomas Bus)
He had the truck painted, at which point he got sick and passed.
The truck remained in storage for 5 plus years
A local small trucking company found, and purchased it, and owned and ran it for a year.
I purchased the truck in February 2014. Moved the axle forward 6"
Swapped transmission for an 18 spd . Bumped the HP up to 525
Then during the winter of 2012-2013 I stripped the truck.
It got: painted, new boxes, pipes, glass, catwalk, fenders, and so on.
I've been driving for about 30 years, OTR for 20. This truck has been a childhood dream to build
I sold the truck (Feb 2018) to purchase a new truck. It just didn't make business sense for the added cost of an older truck. I'll send some more pics of before and after.

CHARLES McKINNON

About eight years ago, we got this '95 international (originally owned by Tri-State Motor Transport) it had been an ammunition carrier with a drome-box. which we removed. 350 Cummins, 9 speed and 4:56 gears when it left my shop it still had the 350 Cummins (we built her up and put the juice to it) but now had a 13 double O/D and 3:73 gears. She was a head turner! We sold her and turned a nice little bit of coin!

DOUG WEEDON Australian Cab Overs

Looks like this is about when Australian truckers realized 'Roo bumpers were a good idea

RAYMOND SCUDDER ------ Rogue river OREGON

Much to be said for trucks with pin striping. Not enough of it being done

My truck still runs daily. 1987 Freightliner, 444 Cummins with 15 spd and 4:10's and 202 wb. Original owner was Bob Wilson trucking, Montebello Ca. Truck pulled a rolling casino trailer and tankers. This truck was the 1st one of 3 spec'd like this. This is the last remaining one and will get it back to original.

SMITH WELLS - Grande Prairie Alberta
Breathing new life into an old Freightliner

Prepped, getting ready for paint
Odometer shows 550,000 miles.

1975 White Freightliner VT 903 Cummins. 320 hp. RTO12513 38000 lb. Rockwell diffs 5.29 ratio 4 spring rear suspension Reyco. Found on Kijiji in Tisdale Sask. It was hauling grain trailers most of its life for an o/o who sold it when the engine failed (coolant in oil). The second owners overhauled the engine and ran it for years, then used it hauling water to their field sprayers. I bought it (blue colour), and wanted to restore it to match the few trucks my dad had years ago in Nova Scotia. I did all the work myself, other than the paint. It runs well and I hope to have it in Reno for the 2019 ATHS show.

BARRY LaFRANCE – aka Bear, Winnipeg Manitoba

Hello my name is Barry LaFrance. Most people know me as Bear. My wife Tracy and I live in Winnipeg Man. We own 2 FLB Freightliners a 98 and a 99. I fell in love with COE Freightliners in '76 when my dad brought the first one home. My dream came true in Dec. 99 when we bought our 98 (big mama). Over the years we stretched her from 210 to 246 wb. gave her a new paint job (thx to Barry's body shop in Rod Holt WI.) different visor ,custom:: deck plat ,side boxes, back window , added dual breathers. We also redid the dash in purple n violet. She's powered by a 525 N-14 Cummins, 13 speed o/o o/o Transmission ,373rear ends on big rubber. She's been my passion since we bought her. In 2012, we added a 99 flb for a winter truck to save big mama. Minni-me is not as fancy. We got rid of the Daytons and put uni mount rims on her, that's about as fancy we got with her. She's powered by a big C-10 350hp 13/o/o ..

GOTTA LOVE THOSE DOUBLE RAINBOWS

Big Mama on a Sunny day

CHRIS CARNAHAN – Huntsville Missouri

Here's mine Ted.
1992 Kenworth k100e
N14 mechanical Cummins
13 speed and 355 rear ends

ABEL GARCIA – Dallas Texas

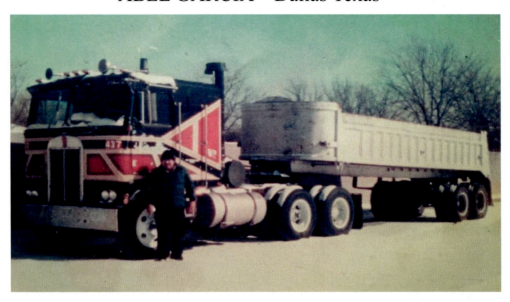

Happy New Year Ted! I seen your post and here's a pic of my dad in the early 80s with our 1974 K100 hooked to a 1977 Lufkin end dump. You have my full permission for use in your book.
Ted Campbell here's my father Abel Garcia Jr. with our 74 K100 and 77 Lufkin end dump back around 83. Not sure if I sent you the pic for your book. Had a 290 Cummins, 13 spd on Reyco spring suspension. Was painted that way when he bought it. Pops said it was one of the cheapest at the dealer.

Pops put a dump bed back then on the Cabover after pulling end dump

MALCOM NAIDOO – Durban South Africa

Hi Ted choose any pictures you want to use.
This is a 1984 MAN 30.321 (321 horse power).
Eaton fuller 13speed transmission. Astas hub reduction differentials.
It's an ADE engine (Atlantis diesel engines) blocks where cast in Cape Town South Africa exact duplicate if the original German engine(6cylinders in line) (engines blocks where cast locally because South Africa faced trade sanctions prior to 1995 because of policy of apartheid).
This truck is currently driven daily here in Durban South Africa by my self.

SEAN HADLEY O'SHAUGHNESSY – WILIAMS LAKE BC
The love of an old truck

Originally from Barkmere, Quebec. Worked in excavation for 5 years where I was taught to drive and operated machinery. I joined the military and spent 27 years serving my country. I was always fan of COE's, my dad had a few and always enjoyed their look. When I spotted this truck in Victoria I immediately wanted it. I approached the owner and asked if it was for sale. He said it's for sale so long that it's not going to get cut up. My plan was to rebuild it and make it an RV hauler. I also wanted to paint a military tribute theme because It is my way of saying thanks to everyone who has served, and still serve. I'm retired in Williams Lake, hope to get on this old girl on the road in the near future.

MIKE HARBISON Sr. Newport Iowa

Mack MH

Mack F 73ST

JIM SKRINAR - Purcell Oklahoma

Thanks Ted, I live in Purcell Oklahoma, this tractor has pulled a lot of trailers
I bought the truck July 4th of 2009 & drove her home 700 miles, she's been the most reliable truck I've ever had & is still ready to go whenever I am..... Shes come a long way since I bought her.
The picture without a trailer is the day I picked her up.

Love a dirty truck
Shows it was out there earning it's keep

BOB ROAD BOSS PETTIT Hartselle Alabama.
Grew up in trucking family.
Alabama State Trooper-Highway Patrol Division.
(Retiring Dec. 2018) Have 25 plus years in trucking.
Owner operator for over 10 yrs.

JASON EVERHARD and PALS

I am based in Woodland, Michigan. The trucks name is "Antique Technique". Now retired, with luck she'll pull her own weight again someday. Until then it's the easy life for her.
1983 k100 3406a 13spd 3.73 Rockwell
I bought it in 2011. Began working it in 2014, retired it end of March 2018
I used it to pull a reefer to anywhere but the east and California.

Marty Miles, Keith Blaylock Jason Everhart, Darin Krause   The ATHS show in Salem 2015

Randy, Jim, Bruce, Glen, Dan, Paul. Myself, Marty, Chris. ATHS Convention Des Moines 2017
Sorry guys! Didn't meet you or catch all your names. But I like your taste in trucks

LARRY DYCK – Newdale Manitoba

1984 Peterbilt 362
3406 Cat 13 speed
3.70 ratio diffs

Nice Winter Scene

WHITE FREIGHTLINER EARLY DAYS AD

1954

LBS LIVESTOCK CARRIERS

They shut down in about 93 to keep a few drivers working Les leased a couple of trucks with H+R

COLIN BLACK – Bellshill North Lanarkshire, England

How about some foreigners Ted Campbell ? I drove this Renault for a few years. It's a Volvo engine 420 power and the 12 speed automatic transmission, Volvo again. The drive axle tyres were just legal when it went to get the speed limiter calibrated. When the new tyres went on it was the fastest in the fleet, and all while recording 56 mph.

DAVE ALDRICH – NEW ZEALAND

A & P Show Ground
Christchurch

JEFF CLOSSON Columbus Ohio
Before and After RESTORATION

HISSON Ohio KENWORTH AD

There's More Worth In A Kenworth
Many would agree

RON BASI – VICTORIA B.C.

In 1977 I was 18 and started working part time at Ideal Fuel and Transport in Victoria BC. My dad Gurdial had worked there since he was in his early teens. At one time, my dad and his two brothers Kirp and Jerry all worked there at the same time. It was the ultimate summer job for a kid that loved trucks and loved to drive. When I was 10 years old, I'd ride with any driver who'd let me. I got to ride in Cabover's and conventional Kenworth's, Hayes, Internationals, Macks, Dodges and Fords. I knew the different sounds of 250 Cummins, 318 Jimmy's, 237 Macks etc. I could identify all the trucks by their exhaust bark, turbo whistle and transmission whines. Ideal trucks not only had unit numbers, they all had names. My dad's 1968 W923 with a 250 Cummins and 13 speed was "E Only Baby". Tony Wraggs drove a mid 60's Cabover KW which was "E Million Dollar Baby" which had a 250 Cummins with a 4 and 4. My uncle Jerry drove it after Tony. Uncle Kirp drove "E Nicest Baby" which was a mid 60's KW Cabover slimline truck and pup set up with a 335 Cummins and a 4 and 4. No air ride, just rubber block or torsion bars. Jim Carvath drove a "2 storey Edsel" which was "E Blue Baby", 220 Cummins with a 2 stick. He later drove a early 70's Hayes Cabover with a 350 Jimmy named "E Go Go Baby". My interest in trucks has been a life long obsession that started before I could walk. I'm fortunate to still be playing with my own trucks today.

THE CARTY FAMILY, JOHN, KEVIN and BRIAN

Our Dad John's '74 with a 375 V-8 Mack on Neway air ride. He came to Canada in '58 from Ireland to London Ontario, worked at Inter City Transport until 1968 when he became a owner operator for Leamington Transport, 1970 to 1980 was on with Kingsway, Paul's Hauling then Greatwest, Day & Ross bought Greatwest out and worked there until he passed away in 92 of Cancer. O/O from 68-92

Our Dad, John Carty's 1970 Mack, 318 Detroit, 13 over on Hendrickson suspension

Brian Carty's 1987 Freightliner, 425 Cat, 13 over, 3:70 on Shaker air ride , 24-5 rubber. Picture taken on the top of 10 mile in BC

Kevin Carty's 1980 Ford 8V92, 15 Over

Kevin Carty's 1980 Ford
After painting
Truck was contracted to
1st Rate, Syracuse NY

Bought my first Cabover in the spring of 1980, age 18. I will always be grateful that Arnold Brothers took a chance and hired me with very little experience.
38 years later I'm still an O/O
KEVIN CARTY

GORD COOPER – CALGARY ALBERTA

My 1987 K100E I bought from Tim Boychuk, who bought it from the original owner & mutual good friend Gord Comrie @ All Canadian Moving Systems. Chris Stelter was the Salesman @ S&M Kenworth, now Greatwest KW, and is still there as PacLease Manager!!

GOTTA LOVE THAT ALBERTA SKY

GORD COOPER – CALGARY ALBERTA

My inspiration to work with trucks and equipment probably came from watching my Dad, Stanley Cooper, plowing Eastern Canadian winter roads, & operating his CAT Dozers, Loaders, and Gravel Crushers. I started my trucking career based in Calgary after nearly 7 years in the Canadian Military Engineers, at several Bases across Canada, including 3 years at CFB Calgary. The lure of Calgary's Oil Business drew me back in 1980 from my last military posting in Nova Scotia, I hired on with Canadian Freightways for almost a year, learning the commercial basics. I started my Hotshot business in 1981 with two One-Ton 4X4 trucks and goose-neck trailers, travelling all over Western Canada & US.

My equipment soon increased in size with the purchase of a new 1985 Kenworth W900 Canadiana Tandem Tractor equipped with a 6.5 Ton Hydraulic Crane.

I specialize in hauling Oversize, Delicate, and Time Sensitive equipment to remote Western & Northern Canadian Oil Rigs, Gas Plants, Mines, Hydro Dams, & Construction Sites. My 1985 W900 Kenworth was traded in on a new 1990 T800 KW, then a 1995 KW, and a 2000 KW, all tandem air ride tractors with hydraulic cranes. I ordered a new Tridrive T800 KW in 2003, mounted a 15-Ton Hydraulic Crane, still operate it, along with my 2007 T800 KW Winch Tractor, and several specialized Lowbed Trailers.

My daughter Melissa, and two sons Matt & Glenn, were raised around my trucking business, travelling and driving, and even acquiring some of my passion. In addition to participating in local truck shows with my kids, I purchased my first vintage KW in 1992, a 1935 Model 89 Conventional, which I restored and still own. My 1957 W925C KW, and 1968 W923 Canadian KW aka "Smokin'Gun" were my next projects, before purchasing the 1987 K100E COE KW aka "Red Baron" in 2005.

Red Baron COE has toured Canada & the US transporting NHRDA Hot Rod Semi World Champion Smokin'Gun to Truck Shows and Diesel Drag Races for more than 12 years. The past 5 years we hauled a live Country Band, and Square Dancing Group in the Calgary Stampede Parade, in addition to commercial Curtainside Lowbed electronic loads in Western Canada. Red Baron also has Pro-Trucker & NHRDA Big Rig Bracket Diesel Drag Racing notoriety, even making it into the 2017 NHRDA Texas World Diesel Semi Finals. Trucks have been my Life since 1980, raised my Family, developed great friendships, provided unique challenges, and even participated in a bit of Diesel Drag Racing History.

'87 KW K100E Cabover aka "Red Baron"

STEPHEN LARGE Czar Alberta

1981 K100C

400 Cummins, 14613 trans Rockwell 40'Son KW Airglide 8 bag air ride

SOME TRUCKS JUST KEEP RIGHT ON TRUCKING
by Stephen Large

Archie Clark and I were at an auction sale in Calgary about 2008 this truck rolled over the block was at about $4000, when Archie started bidding and got it for $4300. He drove it 250 miles home to his shop and had to repair one cylinder in the engine. It sat there awhile until he found a job for it.

He bought a gravel pup trailer, removed the box and hoist installed it on the truck with a sub-frame

which was easily removed from the truck with the box and hoist cylinder intact. He took the truck to Edmonton and worked it at the new Wal-Mart site on the south side of Edmonton. When the job was over, he bought a gravel pup to pull behind it and after a year or so, took it back to Edmonton and worked it at the Terwillegar Wal-Mart site. He worked several jobs with me in the next few years including the Wal-Mart expansion in Lloydminster and a couple of big jobs at CFB Wainwright and the Wal-Mart on the north side of Edmonton. In 2014, I bought the truck from Archie and used it on many of my demolition and construction jobs until early 2017, when I sold it to a farmer in southern Saskatchewan for $10000 without the dump box and hoist. S/N 810059.

TOM HUMPHRIES – New Liskeard, Ontario
My wife's maiden name was Betty Josefowich this is she and her Dad

Betty's Dad Tom Josefowich had a small trucking company in New Liskeard Ont. She grew up trucking. Her fathers company was T & E Rentals. She was a broker for him. Betty went to Toronto Mack to pick up a new truck her dad bought in 78. When she saw the new F model she bought it, 285 Mack with camel back springs, 2 stick 6 speed and about 190 wheel base. Her dad was a beef farmer, in 65 bought a new Ford single axle with a tag & started hauling wood. He kept buying trucks after that all Macks. His last new one in 86 was his 25th truck.
Later she & I ran all over North America with our reefer.

KENWORTH HALF SHACK (Cab-Beside-Engine) PROMOTION

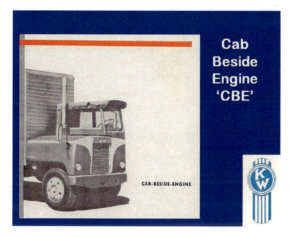

MORE CABOVERS FROM AUSTRALIA -from JOHN KNUDSON
Notice all have 'Roo Bumpers

This truck works in the southern wheat

This is one of mine.

This is another one of mine
parked up at moment awaiting a resto

MORE FROM JOHN KNUDSON

STEVE APPLEBY – Cache Creek B.C.

Well Ted, here's my Cabover pics.

The green and white is a 67, and was my first driving job at Mountain Pacific, flat deck work in BC AB WA OR ID SK. It had a 335 with a married 4&4 and 34 rears.

The yellow was a 74, I ran for Space Trucking out of Ganges from 81 to 86. It had a 350 Cummins, 13 speed, 38 rears, and 18,000 lb front axle. A truck and pup setup with 20 ft decks on each. Hauled primarily for Cubbon Lumber who had stores in Victoria, Colwood, Ganges, and Nanaimo.

The red one is an 80, I had on with I-5 Freight / Salt Spring Freight from 1992-96. It had a 400 Cummins, 13 speed, and 40 rears.

I mainly hauled reefer, bring restaurant supplies from the mainland to Victoria, and grocery supplies from Victoria to the North Island.

BRIAN LAVORGNA - Waterbury Connecticut

CHROME AND STEEL

EVAN GLEN BRENDEL

EVAN GLEN BRENDEL

GARRET THOM

U 85 First Stonebuilt Fire truck

STEVE CONSTANTIN - Ancaster Ontario

CLAIRE GILBERT BRUCE
Mack H Model

JOHN VLEEMIN

My first truck '76 Freightliner, 350 Detroit 6 speed Spicer

MATT FEATHER - Napoleon Ohio

NANCY CAMPBELL

THOMAS MEDIENA
Sketch

ROBERT WHITE

RANDY REIMER - Saint Albert Alberta

Chevrolet

Peterbilt

BILL KRUEGER'S FATHER'S GMC

Jack Krueger was a lease operator with Warren Transport Waterloo Iowa, specializing in agricultural equipment.

MARC MAGLIETTA – Washington, Pennsylvania

Kenworth K-100
Being prepped for painting

MARC MAGLIETTA – Washington, Pennsylvania

HERB MANEY – Pine Glenn Pennsylvania

My 1989 Kenworth K100 French Edition, 60 series Detroit 430HP, 13 speed, air ride 40,000 rears. Former Piper Aircraft tractor pulled their Museum Display Trailer all over America. Part of The Maney collection of trucks. The fairing ,bumper, etc. were called the FRENCH EDITION! I found an old add relating to that nomenclature, couldn't get a print, have not seen it since. Maybe it refers to FRENCHED LIGHTS, like on an old hot rod, to smooth them out, as the bumper and fairing do on this model? The Maney Family has been engaged in trucking, mainly coal, since 1915. 103 years.

A Maney MH Mack, rollin' coal, makin' "the pull"

Trucks in the Maney Collection have to earn their keep.

1993 WhiteGmc owned by Chad Maney, part of the Maney Family collection. It is a true WhiteGMC verified by the nameplate and title. It is 60 Series Detroit 430 powered with a 13 Speed and Neway air ride 40,000 rears. It worked many years and is now used as a show survivor class vehicle.

ED J LEIGEY   Frenchville, Pennsylvania

1960 H67 Mack owned by Edward J. Leigey, Frenchville, Pa. Powered by a 673 Mack, Duplex and single axle rear. It has a 600 Holmes wrecker unit. Now shown as a show survivor class vehicle.

ANTHONY MARTINELLI – New York, New York
Anthony is restoring this 1969 Mack F-700 – 13 Speed
I've done restoration's, they are challenging. Everything electrical, gauges,
wiring. All rubber including the rad and hoses even tires.
Brake system that "looks okay" isn't. First road trips are daunting.

Lots of chatter from truckers that hadn't seen an 8-bag
Page and Page suspension. Anthony found a picture

BARRY SCOTT KEITH - Oregon

350 Cummins, 13 speed

Volvo A & M were an all-COE company.
This was a White, just before they became White/Volvo
This one was 82-83 Cat 3406 with a 13 spd.
Purchased brand new by A.L. Owens Trucking (became A&M in 1989)

STEVE SIMON – San Francisco California

Ted here's an original snapshot from 1990 when the truck was new. Ricky Cepuch found this in his collection. This was at a working truck show and you can see the original combination with the bulk trailer leased to Dirksen, small lettering on the front of trailer.

Ted I bought this tractor April 2015 previously it was owned by Boyd Special Commodities they had it for about 10 years they bought it from the original owner Dennis Saunders of Manteca California. Dennis bought it new in 1990 to lease to Dirksen Transportation. All Dirksen tractors had the same color scheme whether they were owner operator or company trucks. Dirksen was formed by Henry Dirksen and was sold to Gardner Transportation , which was recently purchased by CRST.

COLIN BLACK - Bellshill North Lanarkshire, England

The Brits are innovative, opposing pistons up front and whisky in the barrel

Hi Ted Campbell, I'll certainly pass on your request for more Cabover pics to my buddies, until then here's one I took at a small classic truck show. It's a Commer with a whisky tanker on the back, a lot of those were two stroke diesels, three cylinders, six opposed pistons and a blower to assist with combustion. what a glorious noise they made.

Marc Bridgeman – Peterborough Ontario

MARC DAL PORTO

At first this looked like dust, when I blew it up I realized it was snow.
This tractor shinies up nice.

BRUCE ROCHE – Winnipeg Manitoba

Hi Ted, here is my 199 K100E
N-14 Cummins. 3:70 ratio with a 13 over on tall rubber. Engine was completely rebuilt to about 430hp.
Truck was previously owned by National Mobile Television in Torrence California.
I purchased the truck off an eBay listing in 2006. I use the truck in my trucking operation.
Truck was featured in Overdrive Magazine top 10 Cabover's a few years back.

MURRAY MARIO McKINNON – Charlottetown PEI

The 1981 Marmon Cabover is mine, 400 Cummins, 13spd, 411.
Previously owned by Tommy Johnston of Mars Hill, Maine on with Landstar.

I know it's not a COE but there's something about a Marmon

MURRAY MARIO McKINNON - Charlottetown PEI

1974 Hayes owned by my father, Charles M MacKinnon
335 Cummins, 13 speed, 411 Maritime-Ontario Unit 400.

ALBERT PRIES - Brandon Manitoba

1984 Peterbilt double bunk 3 wiper cab. 400 B white block, 13 speed 3.70 rear ends I bought it in the mid eighties from Peter Wiebe in New Bothwell Mb. I had it on with Keystone Bulk Transport

Manufactured by Amazon.ca
Bolton, ON

26718643R00062